The Battle Tar "Tiger" with the Troops

Wolfgang Fleischer

Schiffer Military History
Atglen, PA

One of the few preserved Battle Tank VI "Tiger," Type B, in the Musée des Blindès (Tank Museum) in Saumur, France.

Photo Credits

1 (Cayé), 1 (ECPA), 26 (Eiermann), 1 (Faustka), 54 9 (Fleischer), 1 (Hagl), 1 (Hensel), 1 (Limprecht), 1 (Schwetzingen City Archives), 3 (Jülch).

Acknowledgments

The author thanks Messrs. Richard Eiermann of Sinsheim, Michael Faustka of Vienna, Ludwig Hagl of Munich, Johannes Heiss of Heidersheim, and Hubert Jülch of Bad Bergzabern.

Select Bibliography

H.Dv.119/328 Shot tables for the 8.8 cm Tank Gun 36 (L/56) of February 1944, Berlin 1944;

H.Dv. 119/329 Preliminary shot tables for the 8.8 cm Tank Gun 43 (L/71)....of September 1944, Berlin 1944;

H.Dv. 470/5f Training guidelines for the armored troops, Vol. 5f: Training on the Tiger Tank, of August 15, 1943; Berlin 1943;

H.Dv.470/19 Firing guide for commanders and gunners of tanks...of August 2, 1944; Berlin 1944;

H.Dv.481/60 Memo for the ammunition of the 8.8 cm Tank Gun 36, of January 8, 1943; Berlin 1943;

D 656/27 The Tiger guidebook of August 1, 1943; Berlin 1943;

D 656/43 Tiger Type B, Handbook for the tank driver, of September 1, 1944; Berlin 1944;

Carius, O. Tiger in the Mud, Neckargemünd 1960;

Katukow, M. E. Na ostrie glawogna udara, Moscow 1974;

Markin, I. I. Kuskaja bitwa, Moscow, no date;

Rokosovski, K.K. Soldatskii dolg, Moscow 1968.

Translated from the German by Ed Force

Copyright © 2000 by Schiffer Publishing, Ltd.

All rights reserved. No part of this work may be reproduced or used in any forms or by any means—graphic, electronic or mechanical, including photocopying or information storage and retrieval systems—without written permission from the copyright holder.

Printed in China.
ISBN: 0-7643-1271-5

This book was originally published under the title, *Waffen Arsenal-Panzerkampfwagen Tiger in Der Truppe* by Podzun-Pallas Verlag, GmbH

We are interested in hearing from authors with book ideas on related topics.

Published by Schiffer Publishing Ltd.
4880 Lower Valley Road
Atglen, PA 19310
Phone: (610) 593-1777
FAX: (610) 593-2002
E-mail: Schifferbk@aol.com.
Visit our web site at: www.schifferbooks.com
Please write for a free catalog.
This book may be purchased from the publisher.
Please include $3.95 postage.
Try your bookstore first.

In Europe, Schiffer books are distributed by:
Bushwood Books
6 Marksbury Ave.
Kew Gardens
Surrey TW9 4JF
England
Phone: 44 (0) 20 8392-8585
FAX: 44 (0) 20 8392-9876
E-mail: Bushwd@aol.com.
Free postage in the UK. Europe: air mail at cost.
Try your bookstore first.

The Battle Tank VI "Tiger" (SD.KFZ.181) with the Troops

In August 1942 the first Battle Tank VI "Tiger" (VK 4501 (H) or Sd.Kfz. 181) from series production left the assembly halls of the firm of Henschel & Son GmbH in Kassel. There were eight vehicles, of which the first, as a result of badly prepared action in the area of Leningrad (Army Group North) had to be written off as losses by the end of August 1942. The "Tiger," until then a well-kept military secret, made its debut in World War II. It was not particularly successful. Other losses followed. A former colonel in the Red Army, I. I. Markin, wrote of this in his book "Kurskaya bitwa" (The Battle of Kursk), which appeared in the fifties: "In February 1943, Soviet troops captured several tanks of this type in combat around Kharkov. The Soviet High Command immediately saw to it that the combat characteristics and special features of the new enemy tanks were examined. On firing ranges and in military science institutions, thoroughgoing tests were instituted with the new types, making it possible to determine the weaknesses and vulnerable spots of these tanks. On the basis of these tests, the Soviet antitank weapons were improved; the Soviet troops received all the needed information about the new German tanks...." All of this happened at a time when the number of Battle Tank VI "Tiger" had just reached the total of 145 (as reported at the end of February 1943). A few tanks must also have been turned over to the Army Weapons Office for testing, which was carried on very intensively parallel to testing on the front. At this time the number of German soldiers who could have become familiar with the new tanks was still very small. Otto Carius, a lieutenant in the 2./Heavy Tank Unit 502 in the war, was sent, as an experienced front officer, to one of the first "Tiger" training courses at Putlos or Paderborn, and reported (Carius, Otto, "Tiger im Schlamm"): "How would the 'Tiger' behave? Its external aspect was anything but beautiful and pleasant. It seemed dull, almost all its surfaces were vertical, only the bow was angled. The avoidance of rounded shapes had been made up for by heavier armor. It was surely not without irony to learn that shortly before the war we had delivered to the Russians the big hydraulic presses with which they were able to make their T-34 and T-43 tanks so elegantly rounded. Our armament experts had placed no value on them, because in their opinion such thick armor never came into the matter. Now we had to accept flat surfaces.

Even though our 'Tiger' was no beauty, its good character could still inspire us. It really drove like a passenger car...."

Meanwhile, "Tiger" tanks also saw action in the North African theater of war. Here they made a lasting impression on the British and American forces. The use of the few available tanks, though, was thus only more divided. By early July 1943, 342 "Tigers" had been delivered, and the real acid test, or at least a part of it, was still to come. According to the will of the Wehrmacht High Command, this was to take place on the eastern front, within the large-scale offensive operations in the summer of 1943. The first goal was the shattering of the strongly fortified front arc around the industrial city of Kursk. Planning for this operation had been proceeding with emphasis since April 1943 under the

A "Tiger" tank is towed to the repair shop by three 18-ton heavy towing tractors (Sd.Kfz.9). These tanks first saw service in mid-March 1943 in the sector of the SS Panzergrenadier Division "LSSAH." During the combat southeast of Krutalya Balka, the I./Tank Regiment "LAH" was supported by a "Tiger" company (Division Order No. 7 of March 5, 1943).

In the spring of 1943, production of Battle Tank VI "Tiger" (Sd.Kfz.181) could be increased to fifty tanks (May). The highest production of 1943 was reached in September, when 85 tanks were completed. The average production time was 14 months, and the price per vehicle was 250,800 Reichsmark.

According to a message from the Inspector-General of the Armored Troops on September 28, 1943, the Battle Tank VI "Tiger" (Sd.Kfz.181) was equipped with combat and loading tracks up to a certain production number. The latter were carried on the Ssyms railroad cars and regarded as part of the equipment. Servicing and cleaning the loading tracks was a job of the armored troops. A loading track had 96 links and was 520 mm wide.

code name of "Citadel." Although a timely attack would have been advantageous, the date for it had been postponed several times. These decisions were based on an intended strengthening of the armored forces, including greater numbers of "Tiger" tanks. When the German attack finally began on July 5, 1943, a total of 146 tanks of this type were ready for service with the two army groups ordered to carry out the operation. They made up some five percent of all the tanks and assault guns intended to take part in "Citadel" on the German side—a ridiculously small number. Modern military history knows only a few examples in which the expectations of the political and military leadership depended to such a degree on the availability of new or higher-performance military technology for the success of a decisive battle. Was the "Tiger" a miracle weapon? Had it been able to fulfill the hopes placed on it in the course of the battle despite its small numbers? This is still reckoned the largest tank battle in history. Let us turn first to the opinions of contemporaries on both sides. The war correspondent Günther Herbst reported under the headline "Far beyond the daily goal!" in the Berliner Illustrierte night edition of July 13, 1943: "Tigers and Stukas stormed ahead on the heights. A battlefield of truly classic form developed before the attacking units....The ideal battlefield for tanks and assault guns, which here—in broad and deep ranks, with the 'Tigers' leading the way—moved forward against the bitterly defensive enemy." A few days later, on July 19, the SS correspondent Zschäckel reported: "The victorious, battle-proved 'Tiger' with its mighty dimensions, with its feared weapons and scarcely penetrable armor, rolls forward between the ranks of attacking grenadiers, mastering every obstacle with ease, to bring death and destruction to the enemy." In another article it was said: "One 'Tiger' shot down 22 Soviet tanks! When enemy tanks prepared to move against the flank of a far-advanced SS armored grenadier battalion," one "'Tiger' quickly attacked the Soviet tanks on hand. Enemy fire was soon directed at the advancing single tank, but the shells bounced off its thick steel plates without effect. Unstopped, the 'Tiger' pushed farther forward, got into a favorable firing position, and shot down six enemy tanks of various types, one after another." It took only a short time for the crew of this tank to shoot down another 16 tanks, including several T-34s.

The descriptions of the combat around Kursk quoted here were taken from the daily press; their value is certainly limited. Yet they agree remarkably with the accounts of Russian participants in the battle, which will not be withheld from the reader. But first a few comments: Including the breakdowns of Armored Units 504 in Sicily and 502 near Leningrad, 33 "Tigers" were lost in July 1933. The greater part of the losses took place during or as a result of the war of attrition on the eastern front. This comparatively low number, to which the losses of other types of tanks and assault guns must be added, compares favorably to the Red Army's very high tank losses. Were the new German tanks successful? Here are the views of their former adversaries in the war. Tank General M. J. Katukov, Commander of the 1st Armored Army in July 1943, reported in 1974 in his memoirs, published as "Na ostrie glavogna udara" (At the head of the main drive), that a talk with the commander of

A totally destroyed T-34 built durintg the winter of 1942-43 is seen on the battlefield in the southern part of the Kursk area. Its armor was 60 mm thick and its front plates angled at 30 degrees.

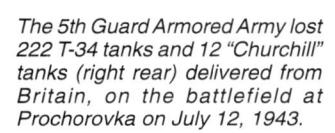

The 5th Guard Armored Army lost 222 T-34 tanks and 12 "Churchill" tanks (right rear) delivered from Britain, on the battlefield at Prochorovka on July 12, 1943.

In 1943 the Red Army received a total of 15,812 T-34 medium tanks. This picture shows the version with strengthened front armor, and with the 76.2 mm F-34 tank gun (1942 model). The gun and its antitank shell attained a penetrating power of 69 mm of armor plate at 500 meters, and 92 mm with the undercaliber shell.

A tank crew cleans the barrel of the 88 mm Tank Gun 35 L/56. The commander was responsible for the proper care of the tank's running gear, radio, and weapons. Major damage was repaired by the repair echelon or the tank workshop companies.

the 49th Tank Brigade, Lieutenant Colonel Burda, on July 5, 1943, inspired Katukov to the following evaluation: "The enemy ceaselessly attacked Burda's sector...with 'Tigers' and 'Panthers' leading....They could not be stopped....We shot at them, but the shells bounced off." The 49th Tank Brigade suffered terrible losses on that day, losing 60% of the brigade. What with these unpromising omens, Katukov received orders on the following day from the commander of the Voronesh front, Army General N. F. Vatutin, to attack the enemies who had penetrated into the 6th Guard Army. He wrote about it: "This task gave us a lot of headaches....What success could be expected from an attack against tank forces that were far superior to us, not only in numbers, but also in arms and equipment....The 'Tigers' with their 88 mm guns could fire on our tanks from a range of nearly two kilometers, thus out of the range of the 76.2 mm guns of our T-34s. Thus, the enemy could fire on us successfully from long range. Did it make sense to play into his hands? Was it not more practical under these conditions to wait with the counterstroke....? We presented our views to the front commander, but until the morning came we remained without a reply....With a heavy heart I gave the order to attack....Our T-34s broke out of their cover, took up their battle formation, and plunged toward the enemy. Armored personnel carriers followed the tanks.

I was uneasy, for I knew what our T-34s could expect from the 'Tigers' and 'Panthers'....The very first reports from the battlefield near Jakovlevo made it clear that our decision had been wrong. The brigade suffered heavy losses."

The man who then commanded the central front in the northern part of the Kursk area, General K. K. Rokosovski, expressed himself similarly: "There were cases in which our tank soldiers had charged at the 'Tigers' in the heat of a counterattack and had been driven back behind the infantry with heavy losses" (Rokosovski, K. K., "Soldatskiy dolg" (Soldiers' Duty), Moscow 1968).

The Red Army suffered heavy losses in both the northern and southern parts of the Kursk area. Some of their military leaders obviously had not known that the Germans, with the Battle Tank VI "Tiger," had entered a new phase in the battle between the effective firepower of the tank and the armor-piercing effect of tank-gun and antitank-gun ammunition. The qualities of the new tank were known to them, but the awareness gained during the battles of July 1943 was not sufficiently taken into consideration. This had its price. The 29th Armored Corps of the Red Army lost 150 of its 212 tanks on July 12, 1943, in an attack southwest of the village of Prokorovka; 117 of them were total losses. In the 5th Guard Armored Army the day's losses amounted to over 300 tanks. A significant number of losses can be at-

Refueling a "Tiger" tank. It took 540 liters of gasoline to fill the tanks. This equaled 27 canisters, or three barrels. With that, the tank could cover 85 km off-road or 140 km on the road.

"Tigers" of Heavy Tank Unit 501 in North Africa. This unit was already being established in May 1942, and in November of that year it joined the German Afrikakorps.

On the eastern front in the spring of 1943. Despite its heavy weight, the Battle Tank VI "Tiger" (Sd.Kfz.181) could be steered easily, even at high speeds.

While on the march, the turret-turning mechanism was protected by setting the turret at the 12 o'clock position and elevating the tank gun to the level of the turret top.

tributed to the fire of the few "Tiger" tanks that accompanied the attacks of Panzer III and IV tanks, opening the way for them with the fire of their long-range 88 mm tank guns. At this point let us hear again from Reserve Colonel I. I. Markin, already quoted several times, who says of the German tank units' tactics: "Again, the tanks moved forward slowly and carefully, opening an extraordinarily heavy fire...." Elsewhere he says: "In this attack, too, tanks of the 'Tiger' and 'Ferdinand' types led the way as a steel shield.... They took the Russian troops' positions under pinpoint fire...." It is no surprise: According to the H.Dv.119/328 "Shot Tables for the 8.8 cm Tank Gun 36(L/56)," the maximum shot range for successful fire on tanks with the 8.8 cm Antitank Shell 39 KWK 36 and 8.8 cm Antitank Shell 40(W) KWK 36 was 2,500 meters. The armor plate of the T-34 (reinforced version) could be penetrated by direct hits on the front armor of the hull and turret at 800 to 1,500 meters with destructive effect, and when hit on the sides or rear even at 2,000 meters. The situation of the KW heavy tank was very similar. The two most important tank types of the Red Army, with the 76.2 mm Tank Gun F-34 (L/41.5) as their primary weapon, could only penetrate front armor under 100 meters and side armor under 800 meters. Slightly better results were possible with the undercaliber shells (comparable to the German Tank Shell 40), which were distributed in small numbers (five shells per tank) immediately before a battle began. The Russian tank crews, to have any success in battle against the "Tiger," had to maneuver their vehicles so that the side and rear surfaces came before their guns.

The new German battle tanks—essentially meaning the "Tiger," for the "Panther" and the "Ferdinand" still showed too many faults in the combat around the Kursk area—made the Red Army work hard despite their small numbers. This finds indirect expression in the memoirs of their military leaders. No book fails to talk of these tanks or stress their importance. It is not without interest that the numbers of destroyed "Tiger" tanks they cite are quite unrealistic. Added up, they exceed the whole year's production of 1943. An examination of the figures given by I. I. Markin ("Kurskaja bitwa") for the period from from July 5 to 12, 1943, gives the totals of 54 destroyed "Tigers" and 36 more abandoned under fire from Russian weapons. These numbers cannot bear factual testing. As already mentioned elsewhere, the total losses for the month of July 1943 are given as 33 Panzerkampfwagen VI "Tiger" (Sd.Kfz.181) tanks.

In the ensuing war years, combat contact with "Tiger" tanks or the destruction of them was always given special emphasis in the Red Army's reports. This was ultimately an expression of the particular threat presented by this type of tank. Yet, at least the "Tiger" I was a makeshift solution in any sense. Let us keep in mind that the development of heavy tanks in Germany up to June 1941 was not conducted out of necessity, but rather from the knowledge that similar designs existed in other countries (The T-35 in Soviet Rus-

"Tiger" tanks were in use at the beginning of Operation "Citadel" early in July 1943, not only in the heavy tank units, but also in company strength in three Waffen-SS divisions and the "Grossdeutschland" Panzergrenadier Division. For example, the "LSSAH" SS Panzergrenadier Division reported having eleven tanks of this type on July 2, 1943.

Two heavy tank units had been established for Operation "Citadel." Heavy Tank Unit 505 (with two companies at first) was with the 9th Army at the north of the Kursk Arc, and to the south there was Heavy Tank Unit 503. The latter was subordinate to the III Armored Corps (Army Group Kempf) and had 45 tanks.

sia, Char 2 C in France). Thus, with a contract dated September 1, 1939, the VK 6501 (H) heavy tank project came into being. With one 7.5 cm 37 L/24 tank gun and two machine guns, it was not more heavily armed than the Panzerkampfwagen IV (Type BW) (Sd.Kfz.161). To be sure, it had considerably heavier armor (80 mm). A prototype was built but not completed. There did not seem to be any appropriate use of it in the armored troops, especially as the campaigns against Poland and France had confirmed the rightness of the tactical-technical concept on which the Panzerkampfwagen III and IV were based. Their operative use indicated higher demands on their mobility than the VK 6501 (H), with its top speed of 20 kph, could have met. Besides, a tank weighing 65 tons only caused problems for loading on railroad cars and crossing bridges. A logical result was cutting the weight in half. With considerably more emphasis, therefore, the development of a 30-ton tank, for which a contract had already been given a year before, was pursued. Frontal armor of 50 mm and a 7.5 or 10.5 cm tank gun, plus two machine guns characterized this tank, with minor variations from Type IV. Four prototypes had been completed in March and October 1941. In May of that year, the Army Weapons Office had continued the request for a tank with 100 mm frontal armor. The result was the VK 3601 (H), of which two prototypes and four chassis were finished at the beginning of 1942.

The year of 1941 brought a fully new situation for German tank armament. Since June Germany was in a state of war with Soviet Russia. At the front, the heavily armed and armored Russian T-34 and KW tanks left a lasting impression on the German soldiers. Among other means of fighting them off, heavy German tanks with strong armament were called for. In mid-1941 the Army Weapons Office had given a contract for a tank gun that could penetrate 100 mm of armor plate at 1,500 meters, without at first reflecting directly on the 88 mm caliber. The request was formulated more concretely in July, when the development of such a weapon on the basis of the 88 mm 36 L/56 anti-aircraft gun was requested of the firm of F. Krupp AG. It becomes clear that the confrontation with the Russian tanks had con-

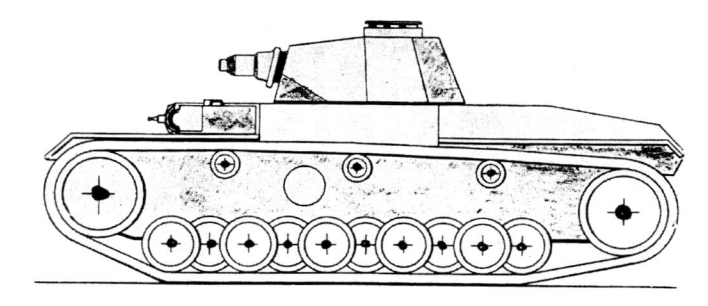

The VK 6501 (H) heavy tank. A fighting weight of 65 tons was intended. The only prototype had 100 mm armor plate (80 mm plate was planned).

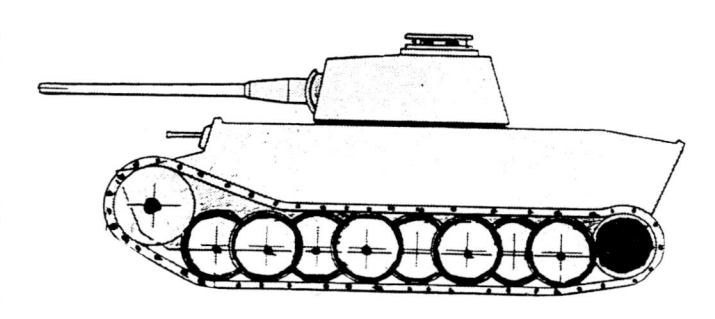

For the VK 3601 (H), with a 40-ton fighting weight, 100 mm armor plate was planned from the start. Its powerplant was a Maybach HL-174 engine.

tributed to the concentration of a goal for what was originally a not very clearly defined request for a heavy tank and its armament within a short time. It had to be successful in battle against a heavily armed and armored enemy.

On July 14, 1943, the "LSSAH" SS Panzergrenadier Division still reported five Panzerkampfwagen VI "Tiger" tanks ready for service. Through the untiring work of the repair service, additional tanks could be readied for service; as of July 15 the number of "Tiger" tanks ready for action was given as eight.

This picture, taken in May 1943, shows the new Panzerkampfwagen V "Panther" (Sd.Kfz. 171) and VI "Tiger" (Sd.Kfz. 181) being transported quickly to the eastern front. With their high firepower and heavy armor, they were to help compensate for the numerical superiority of the Red Army's armored troops.

According to a communique of January 2, 1943, thirty Panzerkampfwagen VI "Tiger" (Sd.Kfz. 181) had been accepted by the Army Weapons Office in December 1942. The manufacture of the 88 mm 36 L/56 tank gun had to be decreased from 25 to 16 in January 1943 to allow increased production of the 88 mm Assault Gun 43 L/71 for the "Tiger" (P) Pursuit Tank.

About one fifth of the total weight of the 56-ton Panzerkampfwagen VI "Tiger" (Sd.Kfz. 181) consisted of the turret with the 88 mm 36 L/56 tank gun. The weapon itself weighed 1.31 tons. The barrel had an average life of 6,000 shots.

Parallel to the first front action of the "Tiger" tanks, this tank was tested at the motor vehicle test center in Kummersdorf. Here many pictures for reports in the press and films for newsreels were made.

The troops always welcomed the arrival of even one "Tiger" tank happily. Their firepower made fulfilling their combat tasks easier for the foot soldiers.

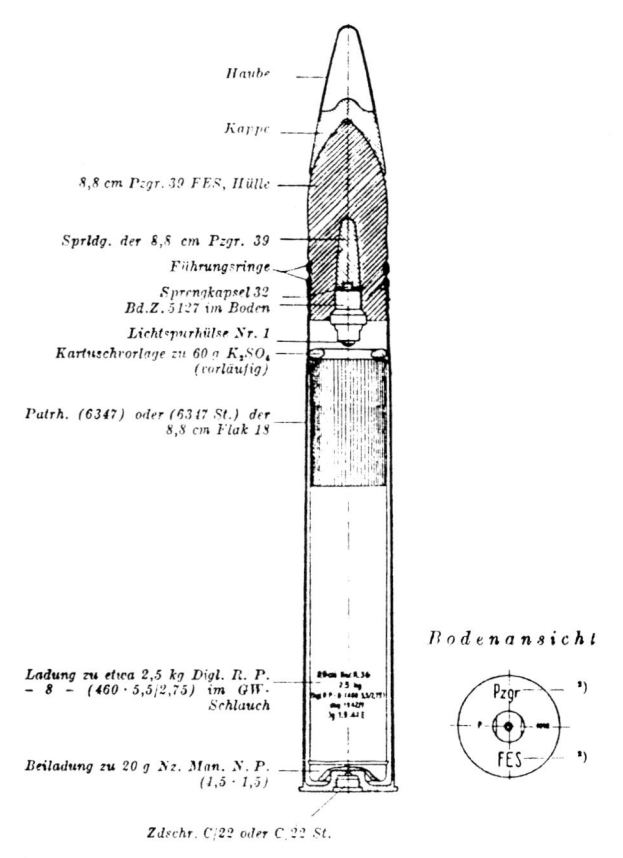

The elimination of the conical-barreled 7.5 cm tank gun (Device 0725), originally intended for the VK 3601 (H), and the necessity of finding room for an 88 mm gun required the enlarging of the turret diameter. The result was a thorough reworking of the 36-ton tank, a widening of the upper hull, along with a considerable gain in weight. The development led via the VK 4501 (H) to the heavy Panzerkampfwagen VI "Tiger" (Sd.Kfz. 181). A parallel development from Professor Ferdinand Porsche's design bureau (VK 4501 (P)) was not put into production. Chassis aleay built formed the basis of the "Ferdinand" pursuit tank, originally designated the "Tiger" heavy assault gun (P), and later the "Elefant" (Sd.Kfz. 184). Great hopes were raised for their utilization in Operation "Citadel," but these could be fulfilled only in part.

The technical development of the "Tiger" has been described in detail several times and does not need to be repeated. It is clear that this tank, as it seemed to dominate the battlefield at the Kursk Arc in July 1943, was a makeshift solution in almost every way. This also explains the dull shape described by Otto Carius. It was known to the responsible parties that it was no optimal solution for a heavy tank. For that reason, the development of an improved "Tiger" tank was undertaken at a very early point in time. In January 1943 the Reich Chancellor and Commander-in-chief of the Wehrmacht, Adolf Hitler, decided that the new "Tiger" then in the planning stages should be armed with the long 88 mm gun. The new weapon had already been

The Tank Cartridge 39 for the 88 mm 36 L/56 tank gun equaled the dimensions and ammunition of the 88 mm anti-aircraft gun. The ignition screw and propellant charge differed.

15

A "Tiger" of the information platoon of the staff company of Heavy Tank Unit 503, seen at Mariupol in April 1943. According to War Strength Memo No. 1150 c of March 5, 1943, this unit had two armored command cars and one tank of this type.

In the summer of 1943 the army's heavy tank units gradually received their final supplies of 45 Panzerkamofwagen VI "Tiger" (Sd.Kfz. 181) apiece. The temporarily supplied Panzerkampfwagen III tanks were given up.

In D 656/27 of August 1, 1943, the crews of "Tiger" tanks were commanded to ford rivers with their tanks. One requirement for this was a hard, firm riverbed.

To spare the powerplant of the Panzerkampfwagen VI "Tiger" (Sd.Kfz. 181), the drivers were directed to drive at 15 to 20 kph whenever the terrain and enemy position allowed (H.Dv.470/5f "Training Instructions for the Armored Troops" of August 15, 1943).

contracted for in November 1941. It was meant to counter the known development of new heavy tanks in other countries. As opposed to the 88 mm Kampfwagenkanone 36 L/56 of the old "Tiger," which could penetrate 110 mm of armor plate at 500 meters with the Panzergranate 39, this weapon, temporarily designated the 88 mm Kampfwagenkanone 43 L/71, provided considerably increased performance. At the same distance, 185 mm of armor plate were penetrated, with 132 mm at 2,000 meters. At the same time, the armor plate was increased (150 mm front surfaces), and its shot-deflecting shape was improved. But the weight was also considerable; it is stated as 69.8 tons.

The first two Type B "Tiger" tanks (Sd.Kfz. 182) off the production line were available in December 1943. They saw their first service on the western front in July and August 1944 (by the end of June, seventy tanks of this type had been completed). In the east, the Type B Tiger first saw action during the combat around the Sandomierz bridgehead in August 1944. According to reports that agree, the Red Army first obtained tanks of this type there. Naturally, their high-performance armament and heavy armor had won them the necessary respect; but the new "Tigers" were not spared losses, either. In action, their heavy weight of almost 70 tons was a hindrance. The problem consisted of getting the Colossus to places where it was able to use its mighty firepower, for the enemy preferred to stay out of its way.

Let us turn back to the evaluation of the "Tiger" tank. Its appearance was evaluated for propaganda reasons by eastern and western enemies. Echoes were given out all too willingly by the German press in order to counteract the generally spreading German pessimism. Number 1 of the "Berliner Illustrierten Rundschaü" of January 4, 1945, under the headline "The Anglo-Americans Call It The King Tiger," provided German readers with a picture of the tank: "From experience gained in tank battles in the East and West, German inventive spirit created this 'super-type' of tank. It represents an ideal combination; on a very heavily armored chassis a newly developed weapon performs. The enemy gave this tank the name of 'King Tiger.' ...The firing results for our previous tanks to date have been far exceeded by the penetrating power of this most modern gun...." Very similar words appeared in an article in the "Dresdner Zeitung" of January 15, 1945, under the heading "King Tiger dominates the field—Germany's newest tank superior to all enemies," one could read: "Not too long ago this 'Tiger' 2 appeared at the front. It was in the west, where it opposed the North American 'Sherman' tank, in particular, and because of its superior armor and firepower created a sensational effect on the other side...." In the "Voelkischer Beobachter" of January 24, 1945, it was said: "For weeks the new Tiger type, the 'Tiger' II, has seen action at the front as the German Wehrmacht's newest tank.... The enemy has named it 'King Tiger' and recognized its superior firepower, armor, and mobility, which, along with other tactical and technical improvements, assure our armored weapon a great advantage over the enemy types."

The Russians reacted more calmly to the appearance of the "Tiger" tank, Type B. General M. J. Katukov, Commander of the 1st Guard Armored Army, reported on the combat around Sandomierz in August 1944: "At that time I saw the heavy P VI/B tank, called the 'King Tiger,' for the first time. The Fascist propaganda praised it in the loudest manner, probably to frighten us or lift the fighting spirit of the German soldiers. With its weight of almost 70 tons, its massive measurements and its armor plate up to 185 mm thick, the 'King Tiger' really made an impressive picture. But as successfully as the Guards fought against the usual 'Tiger' with their T-34 tanks, the 'King Tiger' now knocked them out of the fight; thanks to our newly introduced 85 mm antitank gun, which also penetrated this heavy armor...."

It is astonishing for the observer to see how much the "Tiger" tank has remained a controversial article in the field of publishing, even years after the war. The flood of books, brochures, and articles never seems to end. To attribute that to the name alone—a concept of power and esthetics—would not be true to reality. It would incline to denigrate the achievements of its designers and crews. The former developed this war machine, while the latter did their best to carry out their tasks inside its steel walls.

From a present-day point of view, if one wishes to achieve a final evaluation of this tank, which alongside the Russian T-34 became the greatest legend in the history of armored combat, one must, to be realistic, take two facts into consideration:

1. The small numbers of available "Tiger" tanks. Between July 1942 and August 1944, 1,354 of the "Tiger" I were produced; from December 1943 to March 1945, 489 of the "Tiger" II. In March 1945, thirty newly finished tanks left the factories, plus nine repaired vehicles (including three "Tiger" I). At the beginning of April 1945, the Wehrmacht had a total of 65 "Tigers," of which 48 were ready for service. In comparison, between 1943 and 1945, 3,584 heavy Russian IS tanks were produced.

2. Looking back, it must be said that the heavy armor, up to 150 mm on the last version, and the high-powered tank gun did not cancel out the disadvantages of this tank type's immobility. This is also true of the few special versions of the "Tiger."

A Panzerkampfwagen VI "Tiger" (Sd.Kfz. 181) of Heavy Tank Unit 501 in Tunisia. Each of the two combat companies of the unit was to have nine "Tigers" and ten Panzerkampfwagen III (5 and 7.5 cm guns).

In 1942, 83 "Tiger" tanks were delivered. There were 649 vehicles of this type in 1943 and 623 in 1944. In August 1944 the last six Panzerkampfwagen VI "Tiger" (Sd.Kfz. 181) tanks left the Henschel works in Kassel. The one shown in this picture had the (new-type) commander's cupola installed as of July 1943.

A driving-school Panzer VI "Tiger" (Sd.Kfz. 181) with a propane-butane gas mixture in place of gasoline fuel. Vehicles of this type were used by the "Tiger" Training Company of Armored Replacement and Training Company 500 in Paderborn. At the beginning of March 1945, the replacement army had five driving-school tanks of this type.

The commander of a "Tiger" tank. In the H.Dv.470/5f it is stated: "Only active people of high moral character, who have already proved their complete capability as gunners, are suited to be commanders. Understanding of tactics is a prerequisite."

In the Italian theater of war, the Heavy Tank Units 504 and 508 saw action. After the fighting in Tunisia and Sicily, 504 had to be reestablished, and only returned to service in June 1944. Very little information exists about the service of Heavy Tank Unit 508.

On June 25, 1943, a drill was carried out by the 2nd Company of Heavy Tank Unit 508 in the presence of the Commander of the 9th Army, Generaloberst Model. Cooperation with a radio-directed tank company was practiced in preparation for the forthcoming Operation "Citadel." The 3rd Company of this unit arrived at the front only on July 8 and went from the railway depot right to the battlefield.

"All soldiers are to be accustomed to the physical pressures of tank attacks by being rolled over by tanks, or if not available, by armored personnel carriers or tractors" (H.Dv.298/20c, May 30, 1944). In rare cases, "Tiger" tanks were used for this, as seen here in photos taken by a war correspondent.

In these two pictures the Zimmerite protective coating found on many "Tiger" tanks is easy to see. It was often added later by the crews and was supposed to offer protection from magnetic mines, the use of which by the other side was to be expected.

The 88 mm Tank Gun 36 L/36 was a semi-automatic weapon with vertical breech and electric firing. Its barrel was 4,928 mm long (= L/56), with a maximum range of 10,500 meters. Up to 1,150 meters could be reached in direct fire. Ten shots per minute could be fired. The penetrating power against armor plate was considerable: The 10.2-kilogram Antitank Shell 39 could break through 110 mm of armor at 500 meters; for the Antitank Shell 40 the maximum was 155 mm, and for the 39 HL shell it was 90 mm (all values are valid for a striking angle of 60 degrees).

During the combat at Kursk, the German armored troops turned to the so-called "tank bell" as a new attack process. The heavy tanks moved in the center of the attack formation. In an arc (= bell) extending to both sides and to the rear, Panzerkampfwagen III and IV followed. Behind the "Tiger" tanks moving in the middle, light tanks and armored troop transporters stayed ready for a breakthrough into the enemy defenses.

"Tiger" tanks of the III./Armored Regiment "Grossdeutschland" saw service in East Prussia in the autumn of 1944. The division first fought in the Gumbinnen area, and was pushed back to the Allenstein-Zinten line as a result of heavy fighting.

The crew of a Panzer VI "Tiger" tank (Sd.Kfz. 181) consisted of the commander, gunner, loader, driver, and radioman. They formed "a close-knit combat entity that had to be completely in tune with each other" (cf. H.Dv.470/5 f of August 15, 1943, page 5).

A "Tiger" tank in a well-camouflaged firing position in a rural barn. "Camouflage modified the effect of enemy weapons, decreased their own losses, and thus heightened their own firepower." This principle was especially true of the few available heavy weapons, including the "Tiger."

In the readiness area of the 2nd Armored Division in the northern sector of the Kursk Arc we see a "Tiger" of Heavy Tank Unit 505. It had been taken out of action as corps reserve of the XLVII. Armored Corps on July 9, 1943. At the tank repair shop, the many tanks damaged by enemy fire were repaired.

This tank has thrown a track, and the crew is trying to repair the damage. In view of the off-road track's weight, this was no easy job. The picture was taken in the southern sector of the eastern front in March 1944.

The Panzerkampfwagen VI "Tiger" (Sd.Kfz. 181) could easily overcome dry new-fallen snow to a height of 0.7 meters. In the case of wet or icy snow, the depth could not exceed the ground clearance of the tank (0.5 meters!).

Oberstleutnant Dr. Franz Baeke commanded his heavy tank regiment, which included Heavy Tank Unit 503 with its 34 "Tiger" tanks, early in 1944. In the six-day tank battle near Balabanovka, this unit scored 267 tank kills.

In a firefight the turret was turned by using the turning apparatus, which was powered by a Boehringer oil-fired motor or by hand. When the hydraulic drive was used, the turning speed depended on the rpm of the engine.

In the heavy tank units, repairing disabled tanks was the job of the repair staffs (repair services as of November 1944) of the supply companies. According to War Report 44 (No.1151b of June 1, 1944), a rescue group with two tanks (Sd.Kfz.179) belonged to them.

Otto Carius of Heavy Tank Unit 502 said after the war of the quality of the "Tiger" tank's armor: "Again and again we admired the goodness of the steel on our tanks. It was hard without being brittle, and elastic, too, despite its hardness...."

When "Tiger" units had been in action for two or three combat days, their original strength decreased about 50%. After three more days of combat, only about 25% of the tanks were ready for service. This placed heavy burdens on the workshop companies or repair staffs.

The depicted tank in "The Tiger Handbook," D 656/27 of August 1, 1943, spoke for the quality of the armor on the "Tiger." During the combat at the Kursk Arc in July 1943, it had been struck by 227 Panzerbuechse shots and 25 artillery shells within six hours, and despite extensive damage to its running gear, it had still covered 60 kilometers under its own power.

The heavy armored hood of the "Tiger" tank's engine compartment was 26 mm thick.

This "Tiger" is stuck. Because of its heavy specific ground pressure (1.05 Kp/sq.cm.), the crews were urged to avoid moist meadows with tall grsss, and to take roundabout routes instead. When the tank had driven into such a terrain, it was important to drive through it quickly, without turning or shifting. If it could not move forward, it was to stop at once and be towed out by other tanks or towing tractors.

33

"Tiger" tanks of the last type, with armored commander's cupola (new type) and running gear with rubber-saving steel road wheels. More than 500 of these were delivered, beginning in March 1944. The bottom picture shows such a vehicle from the heavy tank unit of the "Grossdeutschland" Panzergrenadier Division north of Mirau in September 1944.

This series of pictures, taken by the press, was meant to show the public that the "Tiger" tank was invincible. The reality was different. In the "Tiger-Fibel," already quoted, it was stated: "It is better not to smash houses and walls. The stone rubble does better in the newsreel than on your rear end. All the dust is sucked in through the ventilator...."

A contemporary evaluation of the Panzer VI "Tiger" (Sd.Kfz, 181) said: "The extraordinary armor, the great off-road capability, and the outstanding penetrating power of the tank gun allow the Tiger to make a decisive ramming. It defeats all known enemy tanks at a range of 2,000 meters. The Tiger opens the way for the light and medium tanks, or gives fire protection with its long-range gun."

Above, below, and opposite page, below:
Only a few "Tiger" tanks survived to the end of World War II, and today they rank among the most valuable items of military history of their kind in museums and collections. The chance of still finding such a tank is greatest in the vast and primitive areas of eastern Europe. These three pictures of the remains of a Panzer VI "Tiger" (Sd.Kfz. 181) of the last type were taken in the spring of 1997.

A Panzer VI "Tiger," Type B, with Porsche turret, seen at the Vehicle Test Center in Kummersdorf. The turret was taken from the VK 4502 (P); the wooden model of the tank did not progress beyond the planning stage. Fifty tanks were delivered in this form.

The Type B "Tiger" with the Krupp firm's so-called production turret had 180 mm of armor in front (80-degree angle); the side armor was 80 mm thick with an 80-degree angle. The rear was also armored 80 mm thick (70-degree angle). The turret weighed 13.5 tons.

In December 1943 two of the new "Tiger" tanks; the year's production for 1944 numbered 377 vehicles. Another 100 were completed in 1945. The Panzer VI "Tiger" (Sd.Kfz. 181) was used in heavy tank units of up to 45 tanks. In November 1944, a new war strength standard became valid. According to it, the companies received only nine tanks, the whole units 29. Thus, the hope for higher firepower could better be brought to reality.

The Panzer VI "King Tiger" (Sd.Kfz. 182) in action in Hungary on November 15, 1944. The off-road tracks, 0.8 m wide, can be seen. They consisted of 90 links, 45 of them with two leading teeth, while the other 45 were only linking members. According to version, the weight was between 2.8 and 3.2 tons.

A "Tiger" tank with loading tracks (0.66 m wide, weight 1.8 tons per track). This picture was taken during a heavy tank unit's training in the autumn of 1944.

The 88 mm 43 L/42 tank gun had a barrel 6,280 mm long (= L/71). The weapon's weight was stated as 1.605 tons. At 15-degree elevation a range of 9,350 meters was attainable.

The 88 mm Tank Shell 40/43 (without cap and tracer) weighed 7.3 kg and reached an initial velocity of 1,130 m.sec. For the 10.2-kg Tank Shell 39 (below, without contact fuse and tracer) 1,000 m./sec was stated.

The 88 mm Tank Shell 39 for the 88 mm AA Gun 41 (left) and the 88 mm Tank Shell 39 for the 88 mm Tank Gun 43. At 1,000 meters 158 and 165 mm of armor plate could be penetrated.

8,8 cm Pzgr Patr 39 — 1 Kw K 43

8,8 cm Pzgr Patr 39 — 1 Al Kw K 43

8,8 cm Gr Patr 39 Hl Kw K 43

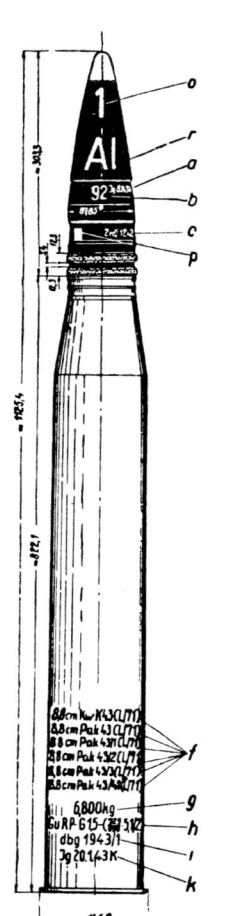

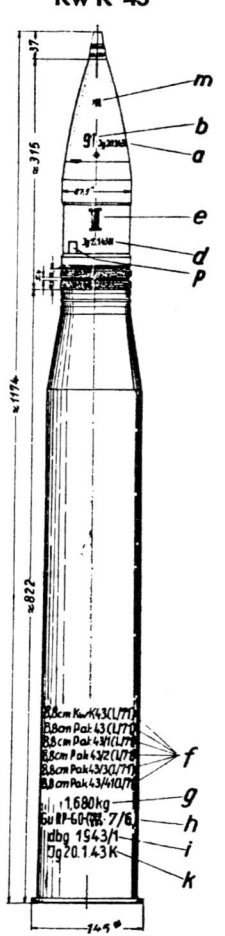

The number of combat-ready "Tiger" tanks in the heavy tank units of the Army and the Waffen-SS was limited. Where it appeared and could utilize its firepower, its crews achieved tactical victories in many cases, though usually without effects on the operative position.

The "Ferdinand" pursuit tank (Sd.Kfz. 184), later called the "Elefant," was built on a modified Panzer VK 4501 (P) chassis. Ninety of them were produced and first used by two tank-destroyer units during the July battles in the Kursk Arc.

Originally, the "Ferdinand" was called "Assault Gun with 8.8 cm Pak 43/2 (Sd.Kfz.184)." In the war-strength report of March 31, 1943, it was called "Tiger (P) (8.8 cm Pak 43)." A tank-destroyer unit then had three platoons of four Sd.Kfz. 184 each; another two of them were for group leaders.

The "Ferdinand" heavy pursuit tank proved to be very breakdown-prone in use. The meager supply of 55 shells was also a disadvantage, as was the lack of a close-combat defensive weapon. The latter was added later.

Removing one of the two Maybach HL-120 engines with attached generator. They gave the 65-ton vehicle a top speed of 30 kph.

In action with Army Tank-destroyer Unit 653 on the eastern front in October 1943. At the end of August it took over all the vehicles of Heavy Tank-destroyer Unit 654, the personnel of which had been transferred to France. In the winter of 1943-44 the tank destroyers were reworked as part of an overhaul in Germany, and in February and March of 1944 they began to see action in Italy.

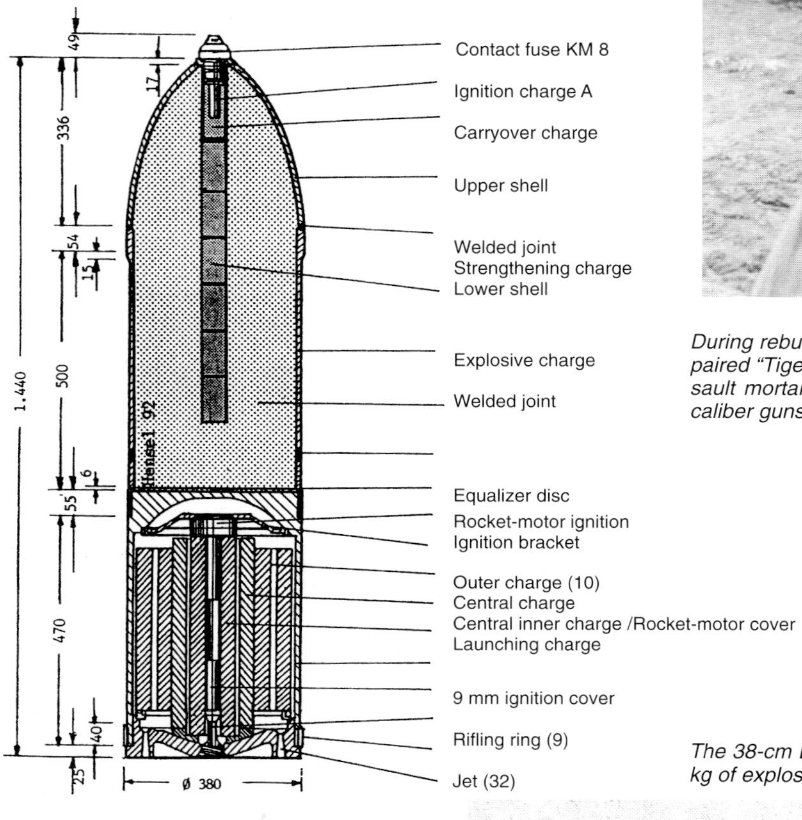
Contact fuse KM 8
Ignition charge A
Carryover charge
Upper shell
Welded joint
Strengthening charge
Lower shell
Explosive charge
Welded joint
Equalizer disc
Rocket-motor ignition
Ignition bracket
Outer charge (10)
Central charge
Central inner charge /Rocket-motor cover
Launching charge
9 mm ignition cover
Rifling ring (9)
Jet (32)
49
17
336
54
15
1.440
500
6
55
470
40
25
ø 380

During rebuilding between August and December 1944, based on repaired "Tiger" chassis, 18 "Tiger" assault tanks with 38-cm RW 61 assault mortars were created to fill a need for heavily armored large-caliber guns to fire mine shells and support the tank units.

The 38-cm Explosive Rocket Shell 4581 had a weight of 350 kg, 125 kg of explosive, and an initial velocity of 91 m/sec.

An explosive rocket shell being fired; its range was stated as 4,600 meters. The 38 cm Hollow-charge Rocket Shell 4592 was also used. It weighed 345 kg. A "Sturmtiger" carried 13 or 14 of these shells.

The heaviest German tank destroyer, the "Jagdtiger" (Sd.Kfz. 186), was first delivered in July 1944. 77 of them were built. This one was photographed in Schwetzingen on March 30, 1945.

LAUDATIO

Born into an old Pomeranian family of pastors, teachers, and officers in Berlin in 1918, he began his military career in the armored troops as an ensign in Tank Regiment 5, and during his further training in 1938-39 he attended the Hannover Military School. Afterward—transferred to Tank Regiment 11—he saw service as a lieutenant with this unit as part of the 1st Light Division (later the 6th Armored Division) in the Polish campaign.

With this unit he saw action until 1943 as platoon leader, company chief and unit commander in France and Russia, and was wounded several times. In 1944 he was summoned for General Staff training, which took him to the staffs of the 22nd Airborne Division in Crete and the XXXVII. Armored Corps. In between he was a tactics instructor at an officer training school.

After the war he wrote articles for military journals, including foreign ones, as well as numerous books on military technology, some of which were translated into English, Spanish, Japanese and Czech.

In the Bundeswehr since 1956, he was first active in training and organizing the armored troops. Later he served in various positions on the General Staff (including in the Federal Ministry of Defense and at the Bundeswehr Command School), and finally as the commander of a Panzergrenadier brigade.

In 1958 his first book was published by the Podzun-Pallas-Verlag. He has written 21 to date. Sincer 1977 he has also written 39 volumes for the Waffen-Arsenal series, which he edits. Since 1977 he has been an advisor to Podzun-Pallas.

Reliable, always cheerful and courteous, he is a gentleman by nature.

Meeting him and being friends with him is a true enrichment of life. His charm and esprit, his chivalry and tireless sense of concealed humor make him a true personality.

Thus, this appreciation is not only a thankful backward look, but even more a hope for many more years together.

PODZUN-PALLAS-Verlag GmbH
Beate Danker and all colleagues,
Rainer Ahnert, Miami FL.